W9-AKK-304

Kids' Guide to Government

State Government

Heinemann Library
Chicago, Illinois

www.heinemannraintree.com
Visit our website to find out
more information about
Heinemann-Raintree books.

To order:

☎ Phone 888-454-2279

⬛ Visit www.heinemannraintree.com
to browse our catalog and order online.

©2000, 2010 Heinemann Library
an imprint of Capstone Global Library, LLC
Chicago, Illinois

Edited by Megan Cotugno
Designed by Ryan Frieson and Tony Miracle
Maps by Mapping Specialists
Picture research by Tracy Cummins and Heather Mauldin
Originated by Dot Gradations
Printed in China by Leo Paper Products Ltd

13 12 11 10 09
10 9 8 7 6 5 4 3 2 1

New edition ISBNs: 978-1-4329-2707-3 (hardcover)
                    978-1-4329-2712-7 (paperback)

Library of Congress Cataloging-in-Publication Data
Giesecke, Ernestine, 1945-
    State government / Ernestine Giesecke.
        p. cm. – (Kids' guide)
    Includes bibliographical references and index.
    Summary: Introduces the purpose and function of state
government, the function of the three branches, how states
raise money, how state government operates, and how a bill
    becomes a state law.
    ISBN 1-57572-513-4 (library)
    1. State governments—United States—Juvenile literature.
[1. State governments. 2.
    United States—Politics and government.] I. Title. II. Series.
JK2408.G55 2000
    320.473—dc21
                    99-057609

Acknowledgments
The author and publishers are grateful to the following
for permission to reproduce copyright material: **p. 5** Getty
Images/©Darren McCollester; **p. 7** Massachusetts Historical
Society; **p. 10** DWR Photo/©Dale Kolke; **p. 11** Associated
Press/©Ted S. Warren; **p. 15** Associated Press/©Bob Brown;
p. 16 Associated Press/©Christina Almeida; **p. 17** Landov/
Reuters/©SHANNON STAPLETON; **p. 20** Associated Press/
©Lawrence Jackson; **p. 21** PhotoEdit/©Richard Hutchings; **p.
22** Shutterstock/©Nancy Kennedy; **p. 23** Shutterstock/©James
M Phelps, Jr; **p. 24** PhotoEdit/©David Young-Wolff; **p. 25**
Associated Press/©Al Golub; **p. 26** Associated Press/©Phelan
M. Ebenhack; **p. 27** Getty Images/©Chip Somodevilla; **p. 28**
Shutterstock/©Brandon Blinkenberg

Cover photograph reproduced with permission of
Photolibrary/©VisionsofAmerica/Joe Sohm.

We would like to thank Dr. John Allen Williams for his
invaluable help in the preparation of this book.

Contents

Some words are shown in bold, **like this**. You can find out what they mean by looking in the glossary.

What Is Government?

A government is the organization of people that directs the actions of a nation, state, or community. A government has the **authority** and power to make, carry out, and **enforce** laws, and to settle disagreements about those laws.

In the United States, the government's power comes from the U.S. Constitution, which was written in 1787. The Constitution is a document that describes, or identifies, the powers of the government. It also places limits on those powers.

Federal Powers	State Powers	Local Powers
Make agreements with other nations	Vote on constitutional amendments	Make agreements with state and other local governments
Provide for national defense	Make agreements with other states and the national and local governments	Preserve law and order
Collect taxes on goods from other countries	Hold **elections**, decide voting requirements	Keep legal records
Print **currency**, **mint** coins	Keep powers not given to the national government	Keep powers not assigned to state or national government

People can band together to let state government know what is important to them.

The main purpose of government is to carry out tasks that individuals cannot do by themselves. These include such things as protecting all the people, encouraging business so that people have jobs, and writing laws that will help people live comfortable lives.

Many nations regard protecting the rights of an individual as an important purpose of government. In the United States, the Constitution lets each person believe what he or she wishes. It gives people the right to hold meetings and express opinions— even if they disagree with actions of the government.

State Constitutions

Under the **federal** system, each of the 50 states has a written constitution. Each of these constitutions describes how the state's government should be run. Each state had to have a constitution approved by the residents or their representatives before it became a state. Many states have written new constitutions since statehood.

The people who wrote each state constitution wanted to make sure that the leader, or governor, did not have too much power. So, state constitutions, like the U.S. Constitution, spread power among three branches of government. Spreading the power is called **separation of powers**. This system has **checks and balances** that keep the other branches from becoming too powerful.

> Vermont has the shortest state constitution—6,600 words. Alabama has the longest—174,000 words. The original Constitution of the United States has only 4,550 words.

Executive Branch

Governor

Carries out the laws of the State

Legislative Branch

State Legislature

Makes laws

Judicial Branch

State Supreme Court

Explains laws

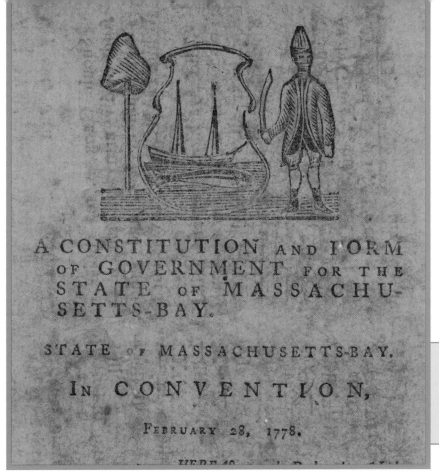

A CONSTITUTION AND FORM OF GOVERNMENT FOR THE STATE OF MASSACHU-SETTS-BAY.

STATE OF MASSACHUSETTS-BAY.

IN CONVENTION,

FEBRUARY 28, 1778.

After its constitution was approved, Massachusetts became the sixth state.

Massachusetts was one of the first of the states to have its state constitution approved by a vote of the people. The Massachusetts Constitution was approved in 1780.

Each state has an executive branch that is led by a governor. The executive branch is responsible for carrying out state laws and for carrying on the business of the state.

Each state has a legislature, which is part of the legislative branch. The people in the legislative branch are responsible for making state laws.

Each state also has a judicial branch of government. This branch includes the court system, which judges actions of the government and the people in comparison to state laws.

State constitutions are much more detailed than the U.S. Constitution. They contain exact descriptions of what state **officials** may do— and how they may do it. In fact, state constitutions even tell how governments of cities and towns within the state should be set up.

State Capitals

Each state government meets in the capital city of that state.
This map shows the location of each of the 50 state capitals.

Be careful not to confuse the words *capital* and *capitol*. The capital of a state is where the state government meets. The capital of New York is the city of Albany. A capitol is the main government building in a capital.

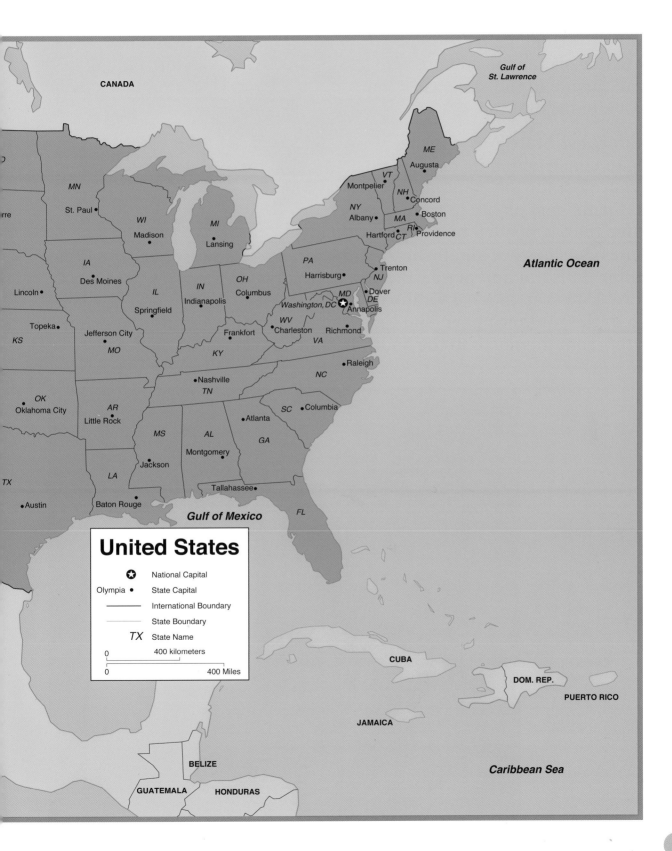

United States

CANADA

Gulf of St. Lawrence

MN
St. Paul
WI
Madison
MI
Lansing
ME
Augusta
VT
Montpelier
NH
Concord
NY
Albany
MA
Boston
RI
Providence
Hartford
CT

IA
Des Moines
Lincoln
IL
Springfield
IN
Indianapolis
OH
Columbus
PA
Harrisburg
Trenton
NJ
Dover
DE

Topeka
KS
Jefferson City
MO
IN
Frankfort
KY
MD
Washington, DC
Annapolis
WV
Charleston
VA
Richmond

Raleigh
NC
Nashville
TN

OK
Oklahoma City
AR
Little Rock
MS
Jackson
AL
Montgomery
GA
Atlanta
SC
Columbia

TX
Austin
Baton Rouge
LA
Tallahassee
FL

Atlantic Ocean

Gulf of Mexico

United States

★ National Capital
Olympia ● State Capital
——— International Boundary
——— State Boundary
TX State Name

0   400 kilometers
0   400 Miles

CUBA

DOM. REP.

PUERTO RICO

JAMAICA

Caribbean Sea

BELIZE

GUATEMALA   HONDURAS

Jobs of State Government

State governments have many responsibilities. Much of what a state does is for the common good, meaning that it is for the benefit of all people in the state. Other jobs of the state protect peoples' individual rights.

California's State Water Project, which began construction in 1957, is an example of a project for the common good. Northern California gets plenty of rain. It gets more water than is needed by people in their homes, businesses, and farms. Southern California is hot and dry. Little rain falls there. However, most of California's people live in the southern part. The California legislators decided to bring water from the north to the south in the State Water Project.

The U.S. Constitution states that laws passed by any state government may not go against any **federal** laws.

The 444-mile (715-kilometer)-long California Aqueduct is part of the State Water Project.

A state worker removes old asphalt from a road. Keeping state roads in good condition is one responsibility of state government.

States build roads and bridges to make it easier for people to do business. State programs help their farmers raise crops. States work to conserve the state's natural resources and increase the annual business in the state. States try to improve their schools. States are also responsible for helping poorer people get medical help when they are sick.

State government deals with crimes, such as robbery, by setting up **guidelines** for the punishment a **criminal** receives. The state also keeps records of births, deaths, marriages, and divorces that take place within the state.

There a lot of work involved in maintaining an effective state government. Therefore, the state employs many people. In some states, more people work for the state government than for any other businesses in the state.

State Government and You

The laws of the state in which you live affect many parts of your day-to-day life.

Sets speed limits on many highways.

Decides what training teachers need.

Tests doctors, nurses, and dentists.

Takes care of open spaces, such as state parks, so you have a place to play.

Issues licenses and certificates allowing doctors, nurses, and dentists to work in the state.

Makes up driving rules for people in the state.

Watches over
insurance companies
to be sure they
provide the services
they promise.

Decides which days
can be holidays
from school.

Pays for building
some hospitals
and universities.

Tests drivers before
they can get a
license to drive.

Runs prisons so you
can be safe
from criminals.

State Governors

Every U.S. state has a governor elected by the people to be head of the executive branch of the state government. During his or her **term** of office—usually four years—the governor of a state lives in the governor's mansion, located in the state capital.

Most governors serve a term of four years. Twenty-eight states allow only two terms in a row. Virginia is the only state that does not allow a second term.

To be governor, a person must meet the state's constitutional requirements. In California, for example, a person needs to be 18 years old, a U.S. citizen, and have lived in California for five years. Other states require that the governor be at least 25 years old.

Governors take a major role in running the business of the state. They prepare the state **budget**. Once a governor prepares the budget, the state legislature votes on whether or not to accept it. In all states, the governor can veto, or reject, laws that the **legislature** attempts to pass.

Governors have to keep a maintain a tight daily schedule to run their state.

JANUARY 10, 2009

8:00am	Meeting about state budget
9:00am	Meet with local farmers
10:00am	Press conference on new policies
11:00am	Tour new automobile factory
12:00pm	Lunch with rotary club
1:30pm	Meet Secretary of State

JANUARY

The governor of a state is responsible for keeping the legislature—and the people living in the state—informed of the state's progress in terms of its budget and other responsibilities.

The state of Idaho often uses television—and a cartoon character named Spuddy Buddy—to advertise potatoes, the state's most important crop.

Besides working on their own states' business, governors often work with one another. They compare how each state solves its problems. They may get together to ask the U.S. Congress for money to help states do their jobs.

Governors sometimes act as **ambassadors** representing their states. They meet with business leaders from other states or countries to encourage them to buy their states' products and to move factories to their states.

Other State Leaders

The executive branch of state government includes other **officials**, too. Most states elect a lieutenant governor who helps the governor do his or her job. If the governor dies or cannot serve out his or her term, the lieutenant governor becomes governor.

Most states also have an elected secretary of state, but the work of these officials may be different. In some states, the secretary of state makes certain that **elections** are fair and honest. He or she also keeps track of official state records, including records about laws passed by the **legislature**. The secretary of state is also in charge of drivers' **licenses** and registration and license plates for cars.

The secretary of state's office is responsible for testing and licensing drivers.

As the "lawyer" for the state, the attorney general keeps the public informed about potential dishonesty from companies.

Executive Branch	
governor	treasurer
lieutenant governor	comptroller
secretary of state	attorney general

Many states also choose an attorney general—the state's lawyer. He or she acts as the lawyer for all the state agencies as well as for the legislature and the governor. The attorney general protects the people of the state from things such as pollution and companies that cheat the public.

A state's educational system is usually in the hands of a person called the superintendent of public instruction, the secretary of education, or the director of education. He or she makes sure that the schools are teaching what students need to know and that school buildings and playgrounds are safe.

Most states have two people who deal with the state's money. The **comptroller** keeps track of the state's money and pays the state's bills. The **treasurer** acts as the state's banker and manages the state's investments and budget funds.

State Legislatures

The main purpose of a state **legislature** is to pass laws. Each state's legislature can pass any law that does not go against a **federal** law or the state's own constitution.

States have different names for their legislative branch. They might be called the legislature, the general assembly, or the legislative assembly. In New Hampshire, the legislature is called the General Court.

No matter what it is called, every state's legislature—except Nebraska's—is made up of two groups, or houses. These houses are often called the State Senate and the House of Representatives or the House of Delegates. The state legislatures work in a variety of ways, but each works according to its own state's constitution.

The main work of a state legislature is to pass laws that allow the state to collect **taxes** and spend money in ways that improve the lives of the **residents**. Important spending programs have to do with health, education, and **welfare**.

In most states, the legislature meets every year for about 60 days. In states with few people, the legislature may meet every other year. Because of this, many legislators hold other jobs.

> Nebraska is the only state with a one-house legislature. Some people feel this arrangement avoids delays and gives voters a clear idea of who is responsible for state government.

> Most state senators are elected for four-year **terms**, and state representatives are elected for two-year terms.

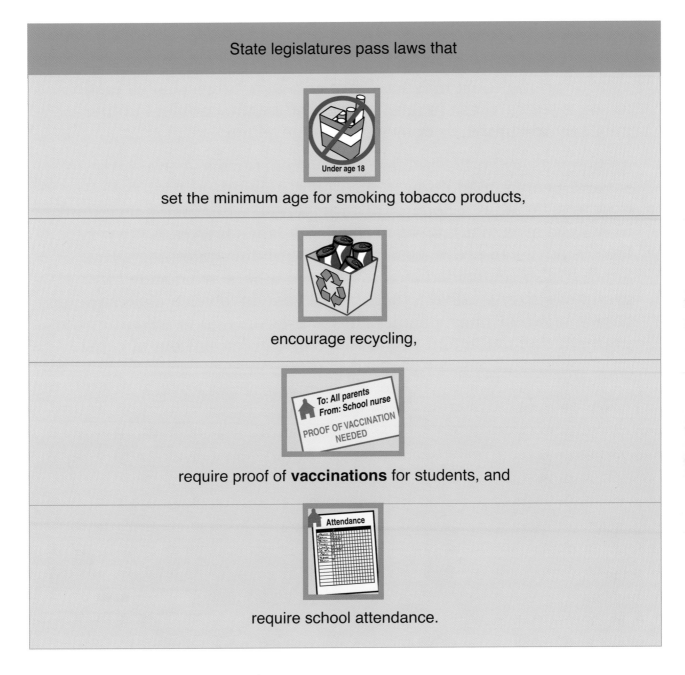

State legislatures pass laws that

set the minimum age for smoking tobacco products,

encourage recycling,

require proof of **vaccinations** for students, and

require school attendance.

Legislatures also pass laws that tell which actions are crimes and how the crimes will be punished. They agree on how businesses in the state should conduct themselves. Legislatures also work with both cities and the federal government to plan highways and bridges.

The Judicial Branch

The judicial branch is the third branch of state government. It is led by the state's supreme court, which explains the state's laws and makes decisions about disagreements concerning the laws. A state supreme court may have five or seven judges, called justices. In some states, these judges are elected by the people. In others, they are appointed, or chosen, by the governor.

As many as 400 other judges oversee court trials. A trial involves several people in addition to the judge. A **criminal** trial, for example, includes a defendant—the person whom the police think may have broken a law—and the defendant's lawyer. A lawyer for the state tries to prove that the defendant did something wrong. Some trials are decided by a judge, and others are decided by a group of citizens called a jury. A **civil case** involves a disagreement between two or more people. These cases only go to trial after the **plaintiff** and defendant fail to reach an agreement out of court.

This criminal trial in Virginia Beach, Virginia, involves a defendant and will be decided by a jury.

In many states, the name of a child involved in a trial is kept secret. This makes it easier for the child to "start over" and stay out of trouble.

States often have separate courts to handle special situations. Traffic courts may deal with speeding and driving under the influence of alcohol or drugs. In some states, there are special courts for people under the age of 18. Many states also have family courts that deal with divorces, parents who mistreat their children, and children who are often in trouble with the law.

Any court decision may be appealed, or reviewed, all the way to the state's supreme court or even to the United States Supreme Court. Cases that reach these top courts usually have to do with the **interpretation** of the U.S. Constitution.

States Working Together

States often cooperate with one another. They recognize official documents from one another. A birth or marriage **certificate** from Michigan is proof of identity in Wyoming. A diploma from a school in Oregon is accepted in Florida. A person who has committed a crime in one state can be arrested in a different state and sent back to the state in which the crime was committed.

States also work with one another when they share a natural feature. For example, states bordering one or more of the Great Lakes decide together how the water should be treated and how much water each state can take from the lake. The Port Authority of New York and New Jersey is a single agency in charge of the bridges and tunnels that connect the two states.

The George Washington Bridge is part of the Port Authority. It connects New York City with the state of New Jersey.

The Colorado River carries millions of gallons of water as it travels through land that is often dry and needs to be irrigated, or watered.

Sometimes groups of states and the **federal** government work together, especially when a valuable resource is claimed by many states. For example, Arizona, California, Colorado, Utah, and Wyoming all work with an office of the federal government as they decide how to use—and how to save—the Colorado River.

Money for Government

Much of the money a state government uses comes from **taxes**. Taxes are fees paid to the government by people and companies for the privilege of living and working in the state.

Many states have taxes of various kinds. The amount of sales tax paid on purchases varies by state. In most states, the tax is a few cents for every dollar an item costs. Some states have sales tax on everything that is sold. Some states do not have a sales tax for food, medicine, or clothing. People who own property—usually land, farms, and homes—pay a tax based on what their property is worth. The more the property is worth, the more the person pays in taxes. Like the **federal** government, some states also use an income tax—a tax on earnings—to raise money.

In 2007–2008, California spent over $13 trillion on business, transportation, and housing. A large portion of this went to building and maintaining highways.

The federal government shares the costs of some roads and highways with individual states.

Fees for using state parks help pay for rangers to keep the park safe and maintenance to keep the park clean.

States also raise money by charging fees to use locations owned or operated by the state. For example, there are fees to use state parks. Some states charge fees, called tolls, for using certain highways or bridges.

States sometimes get money from the federal government, especially for special purposes. Most federal money a state receives goes to education or assistance for poor families. Sometimes the money goes to repair highways and roads or improve public transportation.

Electing State Government

Throughout the 50 states, the **residents** choose who will govern them. They hold **elections** and vote for the person or persons they feel will do the best job.

People who want to be elected governor or to the state **legislature** generally belong to one of two major **political parties**. Most candidates for state office belong to either the Democratic or the Republican party. There are also many smaller parties.

State governments are made up of people chosen by the voters living in the state to be their representatives.

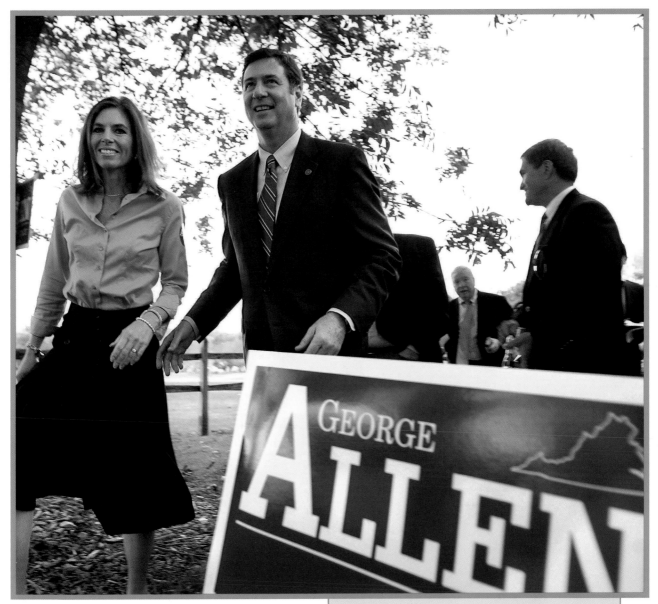

On the campaign trail, candidates try to visit all areas of their state.

Candidates must run for office. This is called **campaigning**. People running for office often travel through a state, meeting as many people as they can. They listen to what the voters have to say about what is right with the state and what should be changed.

There may be disagreements between people living in cities and people living in **rural** areas about what should happen in a state. It is often difficult for a person campaigning for office to please both groups of people. After thinking about the problems and possible solutions, candidates tell the voters what they plan to do if they are elected.

How Laws Are Made

The idea for a law can come from a citizen or from a person already in the state's **legislature**. Either way, both the state's House and Senate must approve the idea before it becomes law.

Students across the country have been directly responsible for some of the laws passed by their states. In Illinois, students wanted their state to have more than a state song, a state tree, and a state flower. They wanted Illinois to have a state insect—the monarch butterfly.

One way to have the monarch butterfly named as the state insect was to have the state pass a law. The diagram on the next page shows the two ways that a bill may be introduced in order to become a law.

Sometimes the people of the state are asked to vote on the bill. This is called a referendum.

Students in Illinois voted for the monarch butterfly to be the state insect.

1

1. Schoolchildren bring the idea about a state insect to a state representative.

2. The representative writes up the idea. At this point, the idea becomes a bill.

3. The bill proposing the monarch butterfly as the state insect is presented to the state's House of Representatives.

4. A committee reads the bill and investigates the idea. They may want to know if any other state has named the monarch as their state insect. The committee reports to the whole House on the details of the bill.

5. The House votes on the bill.

6. If the bill passes the vote, it is sent to the Senate.

7. The Senate studies the bill naming the monarch butterfly as the state insect and then takes a vote.

2

1. Schoolchildren bring the idea of a state insect to a state senator.

2. The senator writes up the idea. At this point, the idea is called a bill.

3. The bill proposing the monarch butterfly as the state insect is presented to the state's Senate.

4. A committee reads the bill and investigates the idea. They may want to know why the children suggested one butterfly but not another. The committee reports to the whole Senate on the details of the bill.

5. The Senate votes on the bill.

6. If the bill passes the vote, it is sent to the House.

7. The House studies the bill naming the monarch butterfly as the state insect and then takes a vote.

8. If anything in the bill changes as it goes through the process, a committee of representatives and senators work out the final wording of the bill.

9. The House and the Senate vote on the bill. If the bill passes the vote, it is sent to the governor to sign.

10. The governor signs the bill and it becomes a law. By law, the monarch butterfly becomes the state insect.

Glossary

ambassador messenger or representative

authority power to enforce laws, command obedience, or judge

budget plan describing the amount of money that will be spent and received during a given time

campaign organized effort to win election to public office

candidate person who wants to be elected to a public office

certificate written proof of birth, or proof of the ability needed to practice a certain profession

checks and balances system that makes sure one branch of the government cannot become stronger than another branch

civil case involves the disagreement between two or more people or groups

comptroller person who keeps track of money that is taken in or spent

criminal having to do with crime, such as robbery; a person who commits a crime

currency paper money or coins that are used in a country

election process of making a choice by voting

enforce to make people obey

federal referring to a group of states that give up some power to a central government, also referring to the central government of the United States

guideline statement of rules to follow

interpretation an explanation of the meaning of words or ideas

legislature group of people with power to make or change a state's laws

license paper that shows that someone is allowed to do something, such as teach school, drive a car, or practice medicine

mint to manufacture coins

official elected or appointed person in a position of power, also refers to any item that is recognized as being legal

plaintiff person who begins a lawsuit against another person or party in a civil court

political party group of people who have similar views about government

resident person who lives in a state for at least a minimum period of time that is set by state law

rural areas that are in the country

separation of powers system of government that distributes power among several branches and keeps each branch separate by making it illegal for persons serving in one branch to serve in another

tax money required by the government for its support; may be based on property owned, money earned, or things bought

term length of time, set by law, served by an elected person

treasurer person who acts as the state's banker; also decides where any money not spent should be kept

vaccination medicine given to protect against certain diseases

welfare providing money, health care, food, or housing for those who can't afford it

Find Out More

One way you can take part in state government is to write your state representative or senator. You can ask for information about the plans he or she has for education or for saving the environment. Find out which bills your representative or senator supports, and let him or her know what you think about them.

Books

DeCapua, Sarah. *Being a Governor*. Danbury, CT: Children's Press, 2004.

Downing, David. *Democracy*. Chicago: Heinemann Library, 2008.

Friedman, Mark D. *Government: How Local, State, And Federal Government Works*. Chanhassen, MN: The Child's World, 2005.

Giddens-White, Bryon. *Our Government: Congress*. Chicago: Heinemann Library, 2006.

Skog, Jason. *Citizenship*. Mankato, MN: Capstone Press, 2008.

Woolf, Alex. *Systems of Government: Democracy*. Strongsville, OH: Gareth Stevens, 2006.

Websites

http://www.usa.gov/Agencies/State_and_Territories.shtml
Find links to your state's government on this site, sponsored by the United States' government.

http://www.kids.gov/
This is the official kids' portal for the U.S. government. It contains links to government sites, as well as fun facts, games, and activities.

http://www.congressforkids.net/Judicialbranch_supremecourt.htm
You can learn more about the court system, as well as the Supreme Court, at this informative site.

Index